# CHARCOAL HOUR

ROHIAYA INTAN HIA

ISBN 979-888546511-3

# Contents

# Contents

# Acknowledgements

We want to thank our readers who are reading this book, our family members for supporting us,our Kashish Publication, our editor, God for helping us in this journey and special thanks to the most important ones, our co-authors, for sharing your moments that you lived.

Thanks to each and every co-author and member of our "Charcoal Hour". We are blessed to have you in our lives. Without you, this book would not have been successfully completed and once again a big thanks to our readers for choosing this book.

# Disclaimer

The anthology "CHARCOAL HOUR" analects poems about darkness and loneliness in their lives. Each writer has presented his/her deep thoughts about loneliness in the form of poems.

The purpose of this anthology was to bring out the feelings people go through alone We believe sharing a piece of our own thoughts through this book might help the readers understand that they are not alone and there are many .people who are feeling heavy and lonely everyday yet not giving up instead picking up their pen to write about them.

Though this is a collection of work of fiction and real feelings of the writers, resemblance of any poem with real life incidents or any person is entirely a coincidence.

# About Us

Kashish Publications is a growing platform for all the budding writers to fulfill their dream. It is founded by Kashish Soni,a budding writer who believe that writing is the magic to heal one's heart.

"*YOU DREAM, WE ACCOMPLISHED!*"

You can contact us for solo publishing or for compiling a one of our own.

Instagram id- @kashish_publications

Gmail- sonikashish004@gmail.com

# About The Compiler

*Rohiaya Intan Hia is a Compiler and a rhymer who was born and raised in Bangladesh. She has been part of more than 60 anthologies as a Co-author and has an aim to increase her participation. Her first anthology as a Compiler is "Seraphic Habromania". She loves to present the gloomy & dark side of life and what she experiences as a human being through her write-ups.*

*A simple candid soul with deep thinking habits, Intan, is also an artist who loves sketching. She holds Bachelor degree of Business Administration and interested to make a great position in marketing & management sectors. Her hobbies include song-writing, painting, choreographing and cooking.*

# About The Project Head

*He is Mr. Krishna Bagdi. He hails from Madhya Pradesh. He is an entrepreneur and a digital business consultant.*

*Founder of Dream World Publication,Dwp Writing castle and Helping Hand Foundation.*

*He has a keen interest in writing and photography.*

*"When you have fire of dreams in your eyes, I am serving you all here so that each writer would be appreciated when someone reads a book."*

# Co-author's Desk

# 1. PRATIKSHA AGARWAL

Pratiksha is a writer continuously presenting her love and thoughts thoughts by penning for last 3 years.
Currently she is studying on Biotechnology and has a goal to graduate soon & reach her destination.
She is a simple girl who wishes to fulfil bigger dreams and let the world know about her magic.

**CAN I BREAK INTO PIECES?**

Can i lose all my anger and let all my frustration come out ?
Can I just stop pretending happy?
Can I cry a loud and say what's going on in my mind ?
Can I betray sadness with happiness?
I wish I could do all these things, but I can't!
Because if I break, my soul will become weak !
If I lose anger, I am gonna lose all my strengths!
If I stop pretending happy , maybe the best people I have will leave!
If I cry aloud, I am going to lose all my mental peace!
And last
If I try to betray sadness then one day for sure happiness will betray me!
Also I can't be the one who betrays anyone for her own cause !
I just want to be the brightest light for every darkness!

# 2. LUCY ADHIAMBO

Adhiambo also known by the pen name Lucia Bentah is a poet who writes all kind of poems. She is also a script writer and a playwright. She basically loves all forms of writing and can challenge herself to write any type of writing. She spends most of her leisure time reading novels.

**HERSELF**

With dark skies,
And grey days,
She decided to look for something,
Which she wasn't sure of,
She just needed something,
To give her reason for living,
She was tired of living a lie,
Smiling all day long,
But crying throughout the night,
Telling everyone she was fine,
But in real sense she wasn't,
She needed something to cheer her up,
Something to bring her real happiness,
Someone to encourage her,
Little did she know that,
That person could only be herself.

# 3. Har Deepansh Bahadur Sinha

Har Deepansh Bahadur Sinha belongs to Lucknow, UP. He is a research scholar of Oceanography and has done masters in Geography from National Post Graduate College. Completed his schooling from Study Hall. His hobbies are art , listening to music , cooking & loads of driving. His interest areas are Astronomy, Writing, Photography & Travelling a lot.

**GOODBYE DEPRESSION**

Don't make your life miserable
When it can be phenomenal,
Though you may be alone
But set a perfect tone.
Stay away from depression
You won't fall for suffocation,
Your life's steering should be in your hand
Fill it with happiness and make it grand.
Society will always spit poison
Work hard for your mansion,
What doesn't matters is their objection
Just five yourself immense relaxation.
Don't consider them in your stories
Since they are jealous from your glories,
They will try to put you down

In tour life they are just clown.

# 4. Mohammed Niyaz

Mohammed Niyaz hails from Mumbai - The City Of Dreams. He often loves to write poetries and short music video stories for his own youtube channel. Apart from this Mohammed is currently working on his upcoming anthologies, as well writing poetries since 2013. You can find him on facebook/mohammed niyaz as well on instagram @niyazsks.

**THOUGHTS OF DARKNESS**

A girl who was at the age of live.
Not having knowledge to think about revive.
Her scars left questions in mind.
Queries that never have been so kind.
The pain she was going through was little bit rude.
Not baring to give chances till mood.
Imaginations and destiny took some change.
In an awful situation of revenge.
However she decided to stand over the fence.
Taking several steps hence.
As far as possible she started living to the most.
From where she's been knowing as lost.
The best friend was her insights.
Which transformed intuitions till bright.
At last she left to minimise the less.
Exiting herself forever from the "thoughts of darkness".

# 5. NOOR TABASSUM

She has participated in numerous anthologies and has also written solo books called Sensibles and Twisted Firsts. She is a nature lover and loves to lead a simple life. She expresses all her feelings in her writings as she thinks it is the most powerful medium to communicate. She has won many writing competitions, and her articles have been published in many magazines too. She enjoys writing poems and short stories. Her stories have been published in the Times of India newspaper too. Her Instagram id is @noortabassumali123.

**LONELINESS**

Though I stay delimited by plentiful people,
Giggling when I am glad but become extinct when I am feeble,
What a calamity is this life, where no one has time to share glitches fatal,
And to live secluded despite being encircled by ample birds like an eagle.
Heart pains and eyes rain blood profoundly,
Infinite tautness pokes the heart squeezing the blood harshly,
Heart and mind pursue relief from the tension quickly,
Eyes try to pursuit for a friend who could share everything, fortunately.
Loneliness is silently killing me conveniently,
Boredom has become an everyday routine unknowingly,
Nowadays, agony is giving pleasure immensely,
I never thought I would face such throbbing days recurrently.

Never know when this water will rise above my head,
Breaking the level of patience and tolerance of the life I lead,
Scattering me into pieces which will then become difficult to read,
And I will then detach myself from the delicate life's thread.
What is the use of the friends who are like a mirage?
What is the delight in being one in a thousand with no usage?
Either be a help to someone solitary,
Or try to be happy without destroying the world you live, cleverly.

# 6. ALI MOYOSORE (KING POESY)

Aspiring to be the best, King (Ali MY) plans to write his name in the sky.

He has been part of many amazing anthologies. Writing is his passion. His favourite phrase is “I don’t know what I’m doing”

**DARK AND LONELY**

Putting a smile on the outside and saying,
I’ll get there if I strive.
Taking the feeling to heart but knowing,
I’ll never make it out alive.
There are thousands of causes for being lonely it seems.
But I’ve been locked in this room by my own self esteem.
There are no doors, no windows,
No chances of seeing the moon’s gleam.
Just walls, just webs,
Just death’s touch to save me.
For me life is just a harsh dream.
I'm all locked up with feeling dark and lonely.

# 7. AFRINA OSHIN

She prefers to read-only. Writing is not the obvious in her characteristics though, hence she has done with some miniatures as she loves to expose my imaginations.

**LATENT DESIRE**

Roaming around my cell
Comes with bursting tear
A mysterious face
A disguised darkness
These bottle up emotions
Toddle with breathing
Touch my leaps with every sip of coffee
Thus, rattlingly write down bucket list
You become deface
Seeming tired
I am not going to vent,
“take a moment here”
Need not confront the warmth again.

# 8. TOOBA TARIQ

Tooba is a student studying in 11th grade. She is from Baramulla, Kashmir. She loves reading, writing, watching movies/shows - anything that can make one escape reality. She has always found words, poetry and books really fascinating. She hopes to master in literature and psychology one day. Writing has always been a pleasure for her. Even though life can be miserable sometimes, she hopes that a better future awaits her.

**GRIEF**

Dark hours of the night
Fierce, loud sound of silence
I look at myself
And feel tragically bounded
My words don't make any sense
My emotions crashed;
I try to wipe the embattled tears of mine
But they don't stop.
I wish things wouldn't be this way
Wish i wouldn't be ruthless to myself
Wish that nothing intoxicating would ever happen
But past always leaves a permanent mark on life.

# 9. Harshita Verma

Co-author Harshita Verma is a writer from Lucknow. She has completed her graduation in commerce stream. She has been writing poetry for the last few years as her passion. She wants to be a novelist in future.

**ALONE**

How it feels to be alone in the world
Like a tree standing in a barren land
No one to support you in the time of need
No leaves on the tree only the stem
No one to smile with and enjoy your day
Not a flower or a bud to give support
The pain of losing everyone in life
Like the leaves falling from the tree
Everything seems lost no hope to rise
Darkness slowly creeping in the mind
Making realise how hollow it is inside
No one realising how it feels like this
Rising tempo of the pain not seen by eyes
The path to darkness it is I know.

# 10. Ishrat Ashraf

Ishrat Ashraf , daughter of Mohamad Ashraf Malik hails from Panzinara Srinagar.Recently completed her Bachelor's degree from GOVT. Degree College for Women Nawakadal Srinagar ,and presently student at GOVT.AMT SCHOOL BARAMULLA. She is passionate writer, debater, painter,social worker Compiler of"SOCIETY "and co author of many books like " From darkness to light","Ravaged souls","Drowned Ink " and many more.
Her pen name is ALFAAZ.

**PEACE**

May be satisfied from our life ,
As others are busy cutting it with knife.
Enjoy your lives with the mash,
Ohh beautiful and may be smash.
Your breaths may be sleeped,
You can be blushed and be weeped.
Life is like a blossom,
May be short and be illusion.
You can always be there,
When life becomes hard and bear.
My rocks upon which I lean,
As the fears passes unseen.

# 11. Muhammed Abdulquadr

Muhammed Abdulquadri Is a budding writer and an engineering student who believes lines are the most suitable form of expression. He has featured in anthologies.

**FRIENDLY DARKNESS**

Everytime I try to speak out my mind.
Their horrible noises cancel it out.
And to their lights I seem to be blind.
Fighting to belong but I am losing the bout.
I don't know the rules to this game of people
So the best I can do is sit and watch.
As they laugh , joke and their vibes mingle
Sharing their fires, I can't even find my torch.
And when it's all over, they put of the light.
I am left with nothing but my own people.
Habiting a couple blocks in the abyss of my mind.
They love me truly and in it we are bound.
When humans are gone ,and the lights are out.
I am left with nothing but the voices in my mind.
Then I stop feeling lonely, I feel more alive.

# 12. Siddharth Mathkar

Siddharth Mathkar is a 17 year old poet who aspires to change perspectives and align lives all over the world. He has achieved the poets laureateship from CSR and runs a poetic blog as well. He believes in the magic of nature and writes poetry for the appreciation of nature and also for major change. Having won several MUNs, he knows how to place a fair argument, and he uses these skills to entrance and encapsulate his readers with his work.

**FALLING**

People change
As falling leaves,
As growing plants
And moving breeze
Yet the sun shall; Constant shine
Upon the fruit that I shall eat.
People move-
As migrant birds,
As seed to plate
And cattle-herds
Yet the rain shall; Constant flow
Down my pleading; Parched throat.
People fade as
A knife's shine dulls
As dying trees,

But you were mine
And yet the apples
Continue to fall; Into the empty garden
You'd call; Yours.
People always
Decay and die
But you are well
And still alive
Only your eyes; Still remind
A shadow of life; That once was live.

# 13. Ankita Nahar

Ankita Nahar, physically she live in AJMER, RAJASTHAN but heartily live in everywhere.

She is too much passionate about writing.

She have always found comfort in words, and that's what attracts everyone. Writing is her therapy, she write what she feels and experiences in her life. You can take a look at her writings on Instagram @naharankita1

**ONCE HE WAS**

Once he was
When it was nice to talk to everyone
Once upon a time they are
Now I feel like talking to myself
Once he was
When I tried to keep everyone happy
Once upon a time they are
Now I try to be happy
Once he was
When the bus was won for others
Once upon a time they are
Now I live for myself
Once he was
When loneliness ran to bite
Once upon a time they are

Feeling lonely now
It's all a matter of time
And when the time comes
Everyone with
Just leaves
So it's good
Be alone be happy
Because when the time comes
This life has gone on.

# 14. Busayree Laila

Busayree Laila is the sweet soul of nature, always caring for others and being gentle with everything she does. She's an aspiring author. She has great dreams to achieve and live a life of peace and success. She loves to talk about various things and characteristics of human life in her writings.

**BLINK**

We feel it creep in
But gone as fast as it came
Loneliness or fear, still unclear
In the empty eyes of the dark
A natural instinct we call it
But our soul says otherwise
For the slight peace it feels
In that quick sudden moment
When it falls into the abyss of nothing
Home, for a split second
It reached home
Then out to the light it comes
But it won't be long
Till we blink again

# 15. Afsana Zaman

Afsana Zaman officially stays in Bangladesh. She holds Bachelor degree of Business Administration on Marketing.
She has been part of few anthologies and wishes to write in more. Apart from writing, she loves to design and draw. Cooking is also one of her favourite things to do.

**EMOTION**

Done and dusted
Two words, thirteen letters.
Easy to say
Hard to explain
My pain spilth in my heart everytime
I have died thousand times
But never fell apart
The darkness of night crush my mind
My loneliness strangle me from inside
But I have chosen you over every crucial things
I want to escape; but I have no wings!
Sadly my hopes stay on the ground
No traces of love nor any light or sound
I want to breath again; out under the sun
I want to grow old with my beloved one
Is it really easy to forget the beloved one?

# 16. Sonali Meher

Hey readers....!! She is Sonali Meher. From - Nuapada, Odisha, India. Currently pursuing for the degree of BAMS at Sri Sri nursingnath ayurveda medical College and RI. She is a Doctor by profession and writer by passion. She started writing when a very special moments come in her life and now for her writing is hobby. The writing is the 3rd person in that way of expressing their feelings, emotions and love. Now get a platform to exploring her writing. Hope ! You guys like it.

**LONELY**

Lonely are the nights
Lonely are the days
Lonely am I, in so many ways
Lonely are the seasons
Lonely are the years
So lonely am I, that it brings tears.
Lonely is this place
Lonely is my life
Lonely am I, that I reach for a knife
Lonely is this court room
Lonely is my sentence
So lonely am I that I ask for repentance.

# 17. Afia Faiza Khan

Afia Faiza Khan, She has been a co-author of more than 12 anthologies and nominated for her writings in numerous American newsletters and magazines. Her praises flies all around that, she is multi-talented, who had won many international prizes across the world regarding her skills, in fact, her artwork has been exhibited in 'Uttara National Gallery' and awarded as the best artist of 'KPRJ' 2020-2021. She is available at:

Mail: lizovi07@gmail.com
IG: dream_19230

**DARKNESS OF THE DARK**

Once I was the regular visitor at a park,
Happy, jolly and always beaming round;
But then happened the worst of snark,
Got abrupt tearing attacks and wound.
Darkness has its deeper dark,
When I was depressed the light smirked,
Darkness hugged me with a remark,
Everything was useless until the loneliness worked.
Without spelling a word monsters turned to bark,
Others wronged yet was thrown with a quirky bound;
That's when I was completely introduced to dark.
Believe me after that I was never found.

# 18. Jhilam Adhikary

Jhilam Adhikary is a student of English in Amity University, Kolkata. She wants to be a poet, writer and professor in future. She is a poet and artist. She wants her poems to change the core values on which the world stands, wishing for a future when people will mind their own business. Her poems have been published several times in e-magazines like TechTouchTalk. You can follow her on Instagram: @d_orange_pirates

**TO THE STRAIGHT MAN'S GAZE**

As soft as heaven; As soft as a dream,
A little jiggly body, and pimples on the skin,
Like the skin of the moon; Who am I? If not beautiful.
A boy without a beard, "not a man!"
If in a dress, or heels: Is a scum,
If with make up and a smile,
"Turn around and be gone…"
For beauty is reserved for the S size waist,
Of a straight, white, woman.
Black, judged, toad skin, mermaid scales, patchy, hairy is ugly.
But the blue-green veins, dehydrated, on a model is preferred and graceful.
Penned down, sketched: Adored, the perfect silhouette,
Too pretty, not pretty, or not pretty enough…
Beholders are blind: They want mannequins, Not humans.

Defined refined beauty: The gaze of the straight man.

# 19. SNEHA DHAMA

Sneha hails to Uttar Pradesh, India. She is a medical student and would like to brief her as aspiring writer. Although not being professional in this field she still loves penning down her thoughts and positive attitude towards the things. All in all will conclude her as writer-- " Being drowned in sea of immense thoughts she found it great to do friendship with words".

**TANGIBLE HEART**

I do take turns
And yet it returns
My tangible heart;
And it's indifferent form.
Non- unless it hibernates
Into misery and songs.
It seeks redemption
But, the hour just moved on .
You don't want to turn!
But aback it's gone.
It's just my tangible heart;
And it's indifferent form.

# 20. Arulmozhi. P

She is Arulmozhi. P, currently pursuing her UG in English literature at PSGR krishnammal college for women - Coimbatore. She is very much intrested in writing poems by her own. She always spread good vibes.She likes photography and editing. She is a positive girl.
You can find her at
Ig handle : arulmozhi_palanichamy
Spread positivity, ignore negativity

**SECLUDED**

Feeling lonely is when,
People close to you,
Doesn't care for you,
And, make the time hard for you;
Moon is also alone,
Paradise your life with moon light;
Sun is also alone,
Ecstasy your life with sun shine.

# 21. Srija Sadhukhan

Srija Sadhukhan is 19 years old girl studying BSc Biotechnology. Love to write poetry and a book worm too.

**DEPRESSION**

From the depth of my skin
Converting my own mind to turn in,
To raise fight against myself
I know you are enemy of my life.
Overcoming depression looks as
I don't belong to this world paths
How to talk about something
Which you haven't experience yet,the suffering?
It's tough to talk about depression
But I wanted to make that confession
Passing through depression somehow
Still believe in overcoming from now.

# 22. Riya Richard R. L

Riya Richard R. L is a young, burgeoning writer in English. She loves writing from her girlhood. Her passion and desire for writing help her to perform conscientiously. She has a unique style and distinct modus operandi in her writings- poems, quotes, short stories, novels, etc... She has worked as a Co-author in 100+ anthologies. She was born in the most beautiful district Kanyakumari in the most prestigious state Tamil Nadu. She is now an undergraduate in Chemistry.

**LONELINESS - A BLESSING**

Loneliness is not a Curse or Pain,
Loneliness is not a Sadness or grief,
Loneliness is verily a Blessing,
It gives unlimited Bliss to you.
Cause' When you're alone
No one will hurt you with false hopes,
No one can cheat you or deceive you,
No one can break you with true lies.
When you're alone, you'll
Learn to be independent and self-supportive,
You won't trust or believe anyone else,
You will develop self-confidence and valour.
Only when you're alone, you can be You,
You don't need to alter yourself for others,
No one can force you or compel you

Most importantly, you have complete Freedom.

# 23. JAGRITI MANDAL

Jagriti is 11. She is an author and compiler.

**THE DARK AND MY MIND**

My mind is moody.

I get irritated.

No control and no longer, stable!

Loving to think and think, think things that are imaginary!

# 24. Manisha

Before Manisha started writing, she got a degree in Psychology from Chandigarh. After that she postgraduate in Development Studies from Indian Institute of Technology, Mandi (IIT, Mandi), Himachal Pradesh.

Some of her favourite works are: Asura (Anand Neelakantan), The Alchemist (Paulo Coelho), A Monk Who Sold His Ferrari (Robin Sharma), The Art of Hearing Heartbeats (Jan-Philipp Sendker) and Butcher of Benares (Mahendra Jakhar)

Her favourite quote: It is during our darkest moments that we must focus to see the light. ~ Aristotle

You can catch her on Instagram @extrovertly__introvert or manisha58680@gmail.com

**NOBODY TO SHARE WITH**

During those days, she felt alone,
even though surrounded by people
in parties, in market, or in mall,
as if she would never be equal
she checked her phone continuously,
might be waiting for a text
she wanted to talk to someone,
but, she found herself perplexed
something was breaking her from inside,
she find it hard to breathe everytime

as if even by thinking about it,
she had done some severe crime
she had a lot of people on her phone,
but with whom to share, she was not sure
that thing was damaging her very badly,
but, till now she didn't find herself a cure

# 25. Bhumika Jain

Bhumika Jain is pursuing her BALLB from NEF College, Guwahati. She is in the first year. She is working as a content writer at Youth Against Injustice Foundation, where she has written various types of content such as Poems, Letters, Short Stories,etc.

**RAPE VICTIM**

Where once there was love, now is only pain,
The whole lot I dreamt, just went in vain.
Being an innocent kid, I was tricked,
When disclose the terror just before humans, I was kicked.
His one step towards me made my life disordered,
Instead of escaping, I decided as to make life well ordered.
Considering all again, I desired to live afresh,
Leaving every single mess.

# 26. Naveen Bhardwaj

I Naveen Bhardwaj a programmer by profession a lover of poetry maker and like reading books and audiobooks and he has a telegram channel @TheNBbook Insta id na.vin7832

**NO CURE FOR LONELINESS**

Loneliness is the other meaning of feeling lost;
Sometimes in family and sometimes in friends;
There is no cure for loneliness; you need to calm down;
Love the people you love, and enjoy the journey with hands down ;
People feel lost; people feel left out ;
Life is not an end there are more things take it with crouch;
Loneliness means different for different people;
For some it may be losing some or losing their hope in something ;
Loneliness hearts the most why is it so;
People count the days; thinking everything will be gone in someday;
They don't know life is a series of chapters you will get your next assignment to prepare for your holiday;
Don't be mad Be even;
After the rain there comes soon rainbow ;
Always give your best; until your good becomes better and better becomes best;
In life you may encounter failure at every path and every step.

# 27. Afrin Ruksar

Afrin Ruksar is a 20 years old Writer and a student of St. Xavier's College Samtoli,Simdega,Jharkhand. Her father's name is Md. Abdul Kayum and her mother's name is Anjum Ara. She has taken English Literature. She is the Owner, CEO & Founder of Golden Letters Publication. And She is a best Motivator, Editor, Singer, Shayar, Poet, Tejasvini Project Member, Founder of Golden Letters Academy etc. She has been an Author of 3 Solo Books and a Co - Author of 140+ Anthologies as well as Project Head and Compiler Also. She is a best helper to the all people. She got the Indian Noble Awards in 2021 to being the best Writer, Compiler, Project Head, Motivator, Singer(Multitalented Person) etc.

**THE LONELINESS**

I lose everyday...
But what to do guys???
Life has its ups and downs, it will keep on coming,
One has to live this life by thinking about it.
I am a human, not a goddess or a god,
I cry everyday then I get silent,
The poisoned cup of life has to be drunk here everyday,
Give me sorrow here on my own,
No one should be disappointed because of me,
Thinking of this, I feel the delicate bond of this relationship,
Always have to sew with strong needles,

To die is the easiest way to get rid of sorrow,
But what to do, my own people always expect me,
Because of this, even from being suffocated from inside,
One has to show everyone happy from outside.

# 28. PRATIK SALUNKHE

He is a Management student. He is a person who loves to write what he experiences and feels. He writes and playes with words in hindi, marathi and english . He loves to be alone in his world but with that he handles and try to keep all his friends and relatives happy.

**LONELY BREAKUP**

I miss the times when you were here,
Telling me to have no fear.
To hold my head up high and strong,
Add happy notes to my sad song.
I miss the way you look at me
As if I were too blind to see.
The path I'm on might hurt and scathe,
But all goes well if you just have faith.
I miss the sound of your sweet voice,
Through bitter times a saving noise
That told me what was right and wrong
But rang in my ears for far too long.

# 29. Adila Firoz

Adila Firoz is a final year student pursuing Bachelor's degree in English. She hails from "The God's Own Country" Kerala. She has won numerous accolades in academic, cultural and literary events. She has worked with a couple of anthologies and has explored the literary arena by getting her poems, essays, short stories and articles published. She has also presented research papers in National and International Conferences. Besides, she is a debater, orator, communication trainer, critical thinker and an artist.

**DEAD CUBE**

It is all so hazy
The world is dark
I fumble I fall
I lie there still
There's no way out
I may better leave
But can I, with all these chains
Pulling me hard?
I don't wanna love
I am afraid to lose
I don't wanna be loved
I refuse to give a dead heart
Survival of the fittest
Tight rat race

I am tired I am done
In a Dead cube I lie there still.

# 30. SHUVANGI CHAKRABORTY

Shuvangi is a 12th grader from Kolkata. A budding writer as well as dancer has strong belief that depression can be set aside . Bad memories or bad days are imminent in ones life but we should not step behind, we have to live our life. Writing and dancing are two forms of therapies which does not let people be lonely. A mantra to be happy is to stay engaged in various activities.

**ALONE**

Trying to cope up
I look up,
To the world of endless stars illuminating the dark.
How unprecedented life is,
How lonely it is.
Apathy is just a common trait now,
Endurance of that character has lingered now.
Amidst the melancholy of darkness no avidity I sense now,
Forgoing everything feels so good somehow.
Away from human race , I thrive now
Long took it for me,
To realise how difficult it is,
But sad reality is what it is.
We are alone forever.

# 31. Ankita Sarkar

Ankita Sarkar is a girl from Jamshedpur. She did her graduation on Hospitality Management and now majoring in Child Psychology. She has published her own book and has been a part of many anthology books. She express her feelings through words.

**LONELINESS**

Loneliness is a world where darkness is allowed,
It is a place of tear and depression,
Where broken heart and soul enters,
With no expectations,
Making them emotionless and make a life,
Jug without water,
Loaded with a gun of sadness,
And take them apart from their families and friends.

# 32. Suchismita Ghoshal

Author Suchismita Ghoshal hails from West Bengal, India. At the age of 23, she has been continuously leaving her footprints in the contemporary literary world. She is an widely published author, internationally reputed bilingual poet, spoken word poet, professional writer, content writer, editor and critic, translator (Bengali, English), performer, communicator and literary influencer. She's been invited to many international festivals and open mics. Her awards, accolades and achievements not only inspire her more to write but also to influence her through the kindness of her words. Her solo books "Fields of Sonnet", "Emotions & Tantrums" & "Poetries in Quarantine" are available on Amazon website.

**FOLKLORE OF SOLITUDE**

Solitude should tear and eat my burning bosom,
I shall draw the speeches of thousand sympathy, originated from the lone-living on my charcoal-black face.
Each page of memories should helplessly jump and surrender in front of the innocent agitation of nostalgia,
They should raid through the dense forest while tracing the stability,
They should choose some exhilarated yet banned adventures,
They should apply ointment of pain-repairing immorality through the warm kisses;
To pay the homage towards my victory,

There's no fault in choosing some inebriating illegitimacy in my narrowed life!
I shall get satisfaction instead of plenitude,
I shall be articulate in loneliness rather than breaking into pieces in love,
I shall count and observe the sensitive mornings
Instead of getting the touch of bewitching evenings,
I shall do my night stay with the thoughts
Of numerous stars instead of having
A peaceful and undisturbed slumber with my head in my darling's chest,
I shall documentize the immortality of solitude Instead of indulging in extreme repentance of failure.

# 33. Priya Das

She is Priya Das, passionate about writing and paintings. She is a trained artist, calligrapher and a published writer. She loves to play with beautiful words and is fond of reading books.Her writings portray a contrast of nature and a glimpse of reality of life .At present she is pursuing Bsc in Biotechnology.

**PEARL IN DARKNESS**

At every night her eyes rolled with tears,
Thoughts are filled with the horrible fear of others.
Her heart is as soft as caramel -
But life is full of pain like hell.
This cruel world filled her beautiful eyes with rage -
But she don't take any revenge.
She wrapped her pain in the silence of her beautiful smile.
No one to endorse except the diary and nature of her life.
She penned every feelings and moments of her life in silence of her diary.
She is the shimmering pearl in darkness....
Fills every soul with calmness.
She was mentally broken still stand up for herself to focus-
On the goal and bloom like a lotus,
in the mud.

# 34. AMISHA CHANDEL

Amisha, a lady who is strong enough to survive alone is this world, is actually broken from within. It's not the love or relationship, but the family and career problem that kills her everyday. She has penned down her emotions in the coming pages. This 20y/o lady has lived a hard life since her childhood, which in turn, has made her brave and strong. She is a management student, and has a goal to 'rule' a reputed company someday.

**WORDS BY A DEAD SOUL**

When my emotions dominate my strength,
my tears spill in this charcoal darkness.
When suicidal thoughts come to my mind,
I wish I was really heartless.
Better is to die than living like this,
wish I could feel the suffocation of coffin.
I'm so fuc*ed up by this tough life,
after death, even my skin will soften.
My anxious thoughts kill me everyday,
it is painful than getting burned alive.
I know how strong I have been,
but now it's getting hard to survive.
My loneliness is deadly enough,
to tear my inner self into shreds.

I've started to love this charcoal darkness,
but daylight increases my sense of dreads.

# 35. SARANSH KUMAR

I am Saransh , from Bareilly . I am a Graduate in Business Administration and a coffee addict. My hobbies are biking and playing badminton and I also love to pen down my thoughts while no one is around to listen me.**MY OLD COMPANION MY LONELINESS**

So again I am back again
From being surrounded by people
To walk down solo
From ordering food for the whole group
To sit and eat alone
From meeting all on weekends
To just sit alone in the balcony of the house
From getting calls on birthdays
To seeing zero notification in phone
My loneliness took me back
From being a person with smile on face
To a person smiling just to hide my loneliness
Betrayal doesn't kill you
But loneliness does.

# 36. Mehak Bhartiya

I Mehak Bhartiya, loves to describe the situations through rhyme poems. Pen and paper had been always there to express my mind in words.

**REASONS STILL NOT FOUND**

I feel too lonely,
and this is sinking me wholly.
Strange feelings around,
Reasons are still not found.
In the Dark sea I am drowning,
And everything's making me frowning.
Of all the time I passed through,
Every single bit is loosing it's screw.
Feelings heavy like these,
Came over my knees.
Surrounded by loneliness,
Where I am a mess.
Is this what life is,
Here seems dismiss.

# 37. Krishma Verma

Krishma Verma is a creative writer by pashion . She has keen interest in motivating the youth about the beauty of life so that interest landed her into writing as she is very found of platable writting. At present, she is pursuing B.sc. in Home Science from the reputed college namely Government Home science College Chandigarh and she also born and brought up in the same city which is afforementioned above.

Her vision is to transform the mind of the person through her writing. For her creative writing is an arduous task, but if certain people aren't with her, during her writing, then the whole writing becomes a very difficult task. She would like to use this as an opportunity to express her gratitude towards these people.

First and foremost, she would like to than God almighty who has showered countless blessings on her. Secondly, she is extremely thankful to her parents who supported and appreciated her in every step of life. Also, she is immensely thankful to her grandmother for always being a constant support. Lastly, a very big thanks to her best friend for motivating her every time and letting her know that she can write.

She owe gratitude to her mother, whose constant support and healthy criticism led her to always think out of the box.

Last but not least, thank you reader for choosing her book. I hope reading this book will be fully enjoyable and valuable for you all.

**WHAT IS DEPRESSION?**

A state when person have no expression,
Want to cry,want to die,
Level of anxiety becomes high,
Overthinking takes place person thinks deep,
Oh, depression don't let me sleep,
Sometimes stop talking, sometimes talks non-stop,
Can I cute but there was no hope,
Freinds and relatives go away,
No one to listen,so much to say,
People think I gone mad,
Stop people it's so bad,
Sometimes happy, sometimes not in good mood,.
Some people behave so rude,
Oh! I don't remember everything is sinking,
People, please change your thinking.

# 38. Pooja Chaturvedi

Pooja Chaturvedi is a Digital Creator from Mumbai, who has an urge to keep learning. She believes in Magic and in Never giving up. She quit Chartered Accountancy studies after meeting with an accident in 2008. In the last decade, Pooja has turned herself into a high-quality, multi-talented personality, by mastering herself as a Singer, anchor, performer, graphic designer, digital marketer, occult, chef-baker, and writer. She is now also a part of a few anthologies.

**I STILL WON'T GIVE UP**

I'm done! I'm done! That's all I have to say,
I'll walk away, the consequences You'll pay,
I'll never look back, I'll never be the same,
I swear I'm gone, it's so difficult to stay.
Your attitude, your behavior, your ways of speech,
I'm crying all the time, why can't you just simply leave!?
I've tried really hard, to get rid of your blames
The screaming, and shouting, and whining all night and day!
The times that are changing are bringing such pains,
It's hurting, its beating, I'm turning to the greys,
I wish there was someone who'd understand my pleas!
I need someone's help! Oh God, hear my prayers please!
I'm done with the sorrows and griefs and all your games,
With no one to help me, I'm alone, with just these pains,
Just wanting to break out of these heavy chains,

To end up my life!- No I won't choose that path of shame

# 39. Charanjeet Singh

Charanjeet Singh is a writer. He live in Kanpur Nagar, Uttar Pradesh. He heartily welcomes you guys to his writing world...

He wants to spread love, feeling through his writing. He is in post-graduate second semester right now and he started his writing to reach out to the people from this year itself...

He also had the spirit of writing since his graduation. Due to study pressure, He was not able to give time...

Now he has reached his destination and he wants you guys to keep learning by smiling...

Hope you enjoy it. Bless his with your big and generous heart...

**POSITIVITY**

Yes

Hope is a big change in life.

I don't have hop and so you can't do anything life because don't believe in yourself.

You are not positive, responsible, problem solving.

Life says you have many questions or problems in your life.

Don't think positive and you think negative, please believe in yourself and believe in your true love or friendship.

So if you have hope and so you can solve all problems. If you have a friend and Family. Your life to change and believe in yourself.

Be Positive. Be Happy

# 40. URVASHI GUPTA

Urvashi (Phoenixxx) grew up in New Delhi, India turned M.T. Initially focusing on performing arts, and life. From her childhood she shows interest in writing and began writing short stories, poems and motivational quotes and many other writings. She is a explorer who love to explore the world in her style. Worked in many companies with different field backgrounds and become the Phoenixxx in today's writers world.

**Feels So Weak Don't (Darkness of our life)**

Feels So Weak Don't
Cause you're just a boy
You know what they say about boys
They say that all we need is violence
But baby, baby, don't we give a damn
I know that you're just a boy
I'm sure that this is how it is
You're a boy, you're a boy, you're just a boy
Just a boy, but you're a boy, just a boy, just a boy
You're not a boy (don't)
Feels so weak (don't)
But you're stronger than steel (oh)
For one perfect performance like at the show
You don't know how lucky you are
When you get the chance

To do it with me
And if you think it's funny
Check out these words I say

# 41. Khyati Sahrawat

Khyati Sahrawat is a 15 year old girl from Dehradun who has always been intrigued by the idea of finding oneself in the midst of all the chaos and confusion that inevitably surface our thoughts. She says that her heart beats for experiencing new things that require her to step out of her comfort zone. In her own words, she loves doing things to feed her soul even if she's not perfect at it ,be it writing a writer bio or the main content itself.

**BLEAK EMPTINESS**

Scared of the human void that surrounds you,
Bawling your eyes out,
All that's there is a broken person in a forlorn crowd.
Tired of the aching nothingness that surrounds you,
You plunge deeper into an inner abyss to search for someone inside,
Bitterness and pain grips you tighter when you realise,
It's empty inside.
Superficially there's so much around
But under the surface there's nowhere you feel safe and sound.
A horrible ,crippling feeling of despair grips you tight,
You sense a hole gaping from the inside.
Your insides hurt under the gnawing pressure from this profound vacuum,
It's all so full yet so empty, all so hollow yet so heavy.
Helplessly running away from the loneliness that chases you,

You're faced with the bleak emptiness and cold walls that surrounds you,
It's you and loneliness in the same sphere on edges quite far,
Together yet so far apart.
Your lungs are deflated of air everytime you face this ostensibly eternal hollowness that hurls you into the dark,
But it's temporary and its a part of a vacant charcoal hour.

# 42. Alina Mohanty

Alina Mohanty, doctor in making and author on progress. She has been part of 50+ anthologies. She is also Vajra Record holder. She is the author of " Realms of Reality". She has her dance YouTube channel. Apart from this, singing and painting fuels up her soul. She is an Empath and healer. She is much more into yoga, meditation and healing.

**INCARCERATED**

The space is reducing,
As if the wall is shrinking.
Shrinking to squeeze out my life.
And block my breath out of strife.
I can't feel my heart pumping,
Neither my veins working.
Still I am living.
Living as if I am no more existing.
This darkness is killing me.
It makes me fell weak.
Defeated and scare to face anybody .
As if I am simply a nobody.
Save me from my devils.
Call upon the divine team.
Send me some magical being.
Save me from being slave to world of grim.

# 43. Azra Zargar

Azra Zargar, is a P.G student hailing from beautiful Kashmir valley, she is having extraordinary skills of writing poetry and prose . Her writings are having essence of postmodernism, romanticism, classical and metaphysical aspects of literature. She is herself a compiler of many anthologies .she has worked as co author in many national and international anthologies under the banner of Notion Press , The Opus Coliseum, Anshay Publication , Shivan Publications etc.

**SINNER**

There is grief in my voice , there is guilt in every moment
Deep in heart consciousness is weeping making lament
Bitterness in eyes , tears of repent and regret rushing down
I am mourning for piousness , I am crying for righteous crown
Soul is at its bitterest grey , feet and mind in sinful world ,
heart is prey , repentance is only ray
Tears rolling down , burning breath , silence deep in the heart
Seeking pardon , seeking forgiveness , as sin was never my art

# 44. ASHAIE FAHAD

Fahad Ashaie, a poet and writer from beautiful Kashmir valley . He has recently completed his pg in English literature from University of Kashmir . He is the post modern writer, but is not restricted to the contemporary period only . He writes in classical, metaphysical, Romanticism, also.

He writes long narratives, descriptives, expositories and pursuvacives.in realism, and reality fiction..and even reaches to magic realism

.and stream of consciousness.

His writing has a taste of a bit of Shakespeare , a bit of John Donne and T. S Eliot. And James Joyce.

He is presently Co Author in many national and international anthologies under the banner of Savan publication , Anshay Publication , The Opus coliseum, etc. He is also the compiler of many anthologies.

**A FAR CRY**

Heard I, a cry far from my emotions,
"crossed have I the rubicons!"
Heeding from the stone blood, yearns who to breathe with gills and walk with fins far away the equators,
Certainly not in the oceans.
"come back from the dead, O Satan,
"Lapsing from ages Am I, the splendid union with Nathan!"

A union, whose seperation, was even, mournful Sophocles felt of, on the river Aegean.
While they failed to retreat Abkhazians, through the English Channel.
Ressurge then, you fire, sand, or water,
Witness the war between Moses and His fraudulent father!
Father! Ain't not You done with the supper?
Along with Jehova's witnesses, sustainable you still, vinci's menacles, reduced to an aggregator.
Joie de vivere! Initial, my consultation,
Comparable, near by, I carnation.
Lately, the flat circles coil the spirals and larger.

# 45. SANIYA MAHEK

She's a clairsentient, a nyctophilic, and a clinophilic soul Who loves to wander and ponder over nature. This is saniya MAHEK, 19 year old from Hyderabad a life science student who is eager to excavate about life. Moreover, her hobbies are reading, scribbling and sleeping. Writing is a part of her life. Besides being a tea lover, she tries new recipes for tea in her free space. She has compiled a book and have participated in more than 8 anthologies.

**ANYTHING IS POSSIBLE**

Broken heart can be healed
Devasted soul can resurrect again
But the pain in brain can never be forgotten
Nevertheless sufferings are confined
Nothing changes until you change yourself
Mere not saying it's the philosophy of life
You find your way to change yourself
Others moulds you as per their business
Which can ruin your peace of life
You change according to you being you
Change the changes of your life which can enhances your business
Thy change can bring goodness to others
Can ruin the conspirators of thy life

# The End

Printed by Libri Plureos GmbH in Hamburg,
Germany

9 798885 465113